APPROACH
FOR OUTRAGEOUS HUMOR!

A lawyer and his accountant are out backpacking in the woods. Suddenly, they spot a cougar twenty yards away. They stand there stunned for a moment, then the lawyer starts removing his pack. His accountant whispers, "What are you doing?"

"I'm going to run for it."

"But you can't outrun a cougar!"

"I don't have to," the lawyer says. "I just have to outrun you."

✖ ✖ ✖

A Philadelphia lawyer is settling accounts with his client. "Let's do it this way," he says. "Pay me $1,500 down and $250 a month."

"Jeez," the client says, "I feel like I'm paying for a car."

"You are!"

✖ ✖ ✖

How does a vulture differ from an attorney? A vulture waits until you're dead before it starts eating your heart out!

LAWYERS FROM HELL JOKE BOOK

Ellie Grossman

A SIGNET BOOK

SIGNET
Published by the Penguin Group
Penguin Books USA Inc., 375 Hudson Street,
New York, New York 10014, U.S.A.
Penguin Books Ltd, 27 Wrights Lane,
London W8 5TZ, England
Penguin Books Australia Ltd, Ringwood,
Victoria, Australia
Penguin Books Canada Ltd, 10 Alcorn Avenue,
Toronto, Ontario, Canada M4V 3B2
Penguin Books (N.Z.) Ltd, 182–190 Wairau Road,
Auckland 10, New Zealand

Penguin Books Ltd, Registered Offices:
Harmondsworth, Middlesex, England

First published by Signet, an imprint of New American Library,
a division of Penguin Books USA Inc.

First Printing, September, 1993
10 9 8 7 6 5 4 3 2 1

Copyright © Ellie Grossman, 1993
All rights reserved

 REGISTERED TRADEMARK—MARCA REGISTRADA

Printed in the United States of America

PUBLISHER'S NOTE
This is a work of fiction. Names, characters, places, and incidents either
are the product of the author's imagination or are used fictitiously, and
any resemblance to actual persons, living or dead, events, or locales is
entirely coincidental.

BOOKS ARE AVAILABLE AT QUANTITY DISCOUNTS WHEN USED TO PROMOTE PRODUCTS
OR SERVICES. FOR INFORMATION PLEASE WRITE TO PREMIUM MARKETING DIVISION,
PENGUIN BOOKS USA INC., 375 HUDSON STREET, NEW YORK, NEW YORK 10014.

For—alphabetically—
Jessica Josell, Molly Katz,
and Henry Morrison

Acknowledgments

Thanks to the following for their contributions: Morris Kantor, Beth Kousagian, Jessica Josell, Dan Tomal, Judy Reiser, Molly Katz, Arthur Indenbaum, Esther Indenbaum, Josephine Novak, Susan Doherty, Joan Goldberg, Kevin Dooley, Debby Reiser (lawyer and stand-up comic), Ellen Stoianoff, M. Lawrence Podolsky, Joe Woods, Debbie Faber, Elise Miller Davis, Roman Calces, Jane Fitzgibbon, Vivian Manuel, Paul Martin, David Margolick, Dr. Julius Shulman, Senator Alfonse M. D'Amato, New York City Congressman Jerrold Nadler, State Senator David A. Paterson of New York, Alan M. Dershowitz, Dr. Rose Oosting, Ronald L. Kuby.

Introduction

Why a book of lawyer jokes?

Please.

Have you ever *dealt* with a lawyer? Do you know anyone who has?

Have you ever passed one on a dark street? Enough said.

Shakespeare got it right when he said, "Before we eat, let's kill all the lawyers," or something like that.

The thing is, of course, we can't kill them. There are too many.

We can, however, heap scorn and derision upon them and *ridicule* them to death.

And that's what this book is for.

For every lawyer whose finagling, finessing, and forestalling put Maalox in your medicine chest, here's a compilation of lawyer jokes calculated to put *him* where he ought to be: growing like an onion, with his head in the ground.

Oh, yes. One thing more. In case you're fearful of offending a lawyer (who knows when you'll need one?), relax: Many of the jokes in this book *came* from lawyers.

There was a terrible tragedy the other day. A busload of lawyers went off a cliff.

And there were two empty seats!

✖ ✖ ✖

A lawyer named Sam and his accountant are backpacking in the woods. Suddenly, they spot a cougar 20 yards away. They stand there stunned for a moment, then Sam starts removing his pack.

His accountant whispers, "What are you doing?"

"I'm going to run for it."

"But you can't outrun a cougar!"

"I don't have to," Sam says. "I just have to outrun you!"

✖ ✖ ✖

What do you call the fees of an inexperienced lawyer? Small graft warning!

✖ ✖ ✖

What's the difference between a catfish and a lawyer? One is a scum-sucking, bottom-feeding scavenger. The other is a fish!

✖ ✖ ✖

A doctor and his lawyer, Manny, go golfing on Long Island. At the tenth hole, the doctor gets hit smack on the head with a wild golf ball.

Immediately, the errant golfer rushes over. "I'm so sorry! Are you all right?"

The doctor starts to say, "I'm fine," when Manny jumps in. "All right? Look at the lump on his head! We want a check for five thousand dollars or we're taking you to court!"

The errant golfer says, "But I hollered, 'Fore!' "

At which point, Manny shakes the golfer's hand and says, "It's a deal!"

✖ ✖ ✖

Did you hear how Justice Clarence Thomas greeted his new colleagues on the Supreme Court? "How do you do? How do you do? How do you do? Nice boobs. How do you do? . . ."

✖ ✖ ✖

Talk about justice. My cousin's lawyer finally wound up in jail for making big money. It was a quarter of an inch too long!

✖ ✖ ✖

A lawyer is boasting to his girlfriend about a big divorce settlement he just pulled off for his client Arnold. "I hired a guy to plant marijuana in the wife's car and tipped off the cops. Then I bribed a bartender to swear she spent every night drinking till dawn. In the end, Arnold got custody of the kids, the house, both cars, and his wife got absolutely nothing!"

The girlfriend frowns and says, "Really, Tom. Where's your self-respect?"

"I threw that in to close the deal!"

✖ ✖ ✖

A Philadelphia lawyer named Ira is settling accounts with his client. "Let's do it this way," Ira says. "Pay me fifteen hundred down and two-fifty a month."

"Jeez," the client says. "I feel like I'm paying for a car."

"You are!"

✖ ✖ ✖

Not all lawyers are scum. I know one who stopped cheating his clients and lying to juries on the very same day.

It was a beautiful funeral!

✖ ✖ ✖

A doctor, an engineer, and a lawyer are arguing over who owns the smartest dog. The doctor says, "I know how to settle it." He tosses a pile of bones into the middle of the room, then he whispers into his poodle, Scalpel's, ear. The dog races over to the bones and, in three minutes, constructs a perfect human skeleton.

"You think that's something?" the engineer sneers. He calls over his fox terrier, Slide-rule, gives him instructions, and in just two minutes, Slide-rule builds a flawless suspension bridge out of the bones.

At this point, the lawyer takes his pit bull, Loophole, into a corner, says a few words, and in thirty seconds, Loophole screws the other two dogs and takes the rest of the day off!

✖ ✖ ✖

How can you tell a snake from a lawyer?
A snake keeps dropping the briefcase!

✖ ✖ ✖

Lucifer and St. Peter agree to divide the cost of a fax machine to send messages between Heaven and Hell. To test the machine, St. Peter faxes Lucifer a copy of the bill with a note: "Thank you for your attention to this matter."

Lucifer ignores it, so St. Peter sends a polite reminder.

Still, no response.

Finally, St. Peter stomps down to Hell and marches into Lucifer's office. He slaps the bill on Lucifer's desk and snaps, "We agreed to split the cost of that fax machine, but so far you haven't paid one dime. If you don't make good, I'm going to haul you into court and sue the pants off you!"

Lucifer lights a cigar with his finger, takes a puff, and says, "No, you won't."

St. Peter glares. "Oh, no? What makes you think so?"

"Give me a break—where're you going to find a lawyer?"

✖ ✖ ✖

What do you get when you cross the Godfather with a lawyer? An offer you can't understand!

✖ ✖ ✖

A blind snake meets a blind rabbit in the middle of the road. To determine what kind of creature he's come across, the snake coils itself around the rabbit. "Hm. You're warm and fluffy. You've got long ears and a nose that twitches. You must be a bunny rabbit!"

"Right!" the rabbit says. "Now let me see if I can figure out what you are." With that, the rabbit runs his paws over the snake. He thinks for a while. Finally, the rabbit says, "You're cold and slimy, and you've got a forked tongue. You gotta be a lawyer!"

✖ ✖ ✖

I asked my lawyer for a hand. It's been in my wallet ever since!

✖ ✖ ✖

A prominent Boston divorce lawyer dies. At the funeral, one of the mourners is sobbing uncontrollably. A friend comes over and says, "Well, at least Calvin died peacefully, of natural causes."

"That's just it," the mourner cries. "I wanted to see him hanged!"

✖ ✖ ✖

What do you call it when a lawyer is up to his neck in cement? Not enough cement!

✖ ✖ ✖

A minister, an environmentalist, and a lawyer named Randolph find themselves at the Pearly Gates. The angel in charge takes the minister aside and says, "Before you can enter, I've got to ask you to add two and two."

"I understand," the minister says. "The answer is four."

"Pass through," the angel says, and moves on to the environmentalist."

"Just a formality," he says. "Please divide three into nine."

"Sure," the environmentalist says. "You get three."

"Good," the angel says, and turns to the lawyer. He begins, "I can't let you in until you undergo this little test—"

Furious, Randolph interrupts him. "I've had it! Just because I'm a lawyer, everybody's got it in for me. I'm dead, for God's sake. Give me a break!"

"Look," the angel says. "It's nothing personal. I don't make the rules. Everybody's got to pass a test."

Randolph sniffs and says, "All right. What's the question?"

"How much is 1497.03 times 846?"

✖ ✖ ✖

My lawyer is never bothered by his conscience. It doesn't speak his language!

✖ ✖ ✖

What do you call 200 lawyers at the bottom of Chesapeake Bay? A good beginning!

✖ ✖ ✖

As soon as the verdict is announced, a young lawyer named Will rushes out of the courtroom and calls the senior partner of his law firm.

"What happened?" the partner asks.

"Justice prevailed."

"Good grief," the partner hollers. "Appeal! Appeal!"

✖ ✖ ✖

How does a vulture differ from an attorney?

A vulture waits until you're dead before it starts eating your heart out!

✖ ✖ ✖

Definition of a lawyer: a guy who helps you get what's coming to him!

✖ ✖ ✖

"Don't forget: Appearances are everything," the senior partner tells George, the new lawyer in the firm. "Yes, sir," George responds and goes off to his office. Since this is his first day on the job, he's got nothing to do, so he shuffles paper and sorts paper clips.

Finally, to his relief, George sees his secretary approaching with his first client. As they enter, George grabs his phone and snaps, "Look, Trump, I've told you a dozen times, I can't possibly go over that deal for at least another week. I'm just too swamped. Give me a call in ten days and I'll see what I can do."

With a flourish, he hangs up the phone and regards the man standing before him. "Is there something I can do for you?" George says, coolly.

"No. I just stopped by to hook up your phone."

✗ ✗ ✗

Did you hear they're now using lawyers instead of rats in laboratory experiments?

Well, think about it. There are more lawyers

than rats. You don't become as attached to a lawyer as you do a rat. And lawyers will do things rats won't!

✖ ✖ ✖

A lawyer's life begins with a tiny cell. And if there was any justice, it would end there, too!

✖ ✖ ✖

At an Upper East Side cocktail party, Harry the lawyer runs into a chiropractor.

"I've been having trouble with my back," Harry says. "I can't sleep at night. Which side do you think I should lie on?"

The chiropractor replies, "The one that comes up with the retainer!"

✖ ✖ ✖

What's the difference between an attorney and an indigant hen? An indignant hen clucks defiance!

✖ ✖ ✖

Did you hear about the lawyer who broke up with his fiancée? First, he made her return the ring. Then he billed her for 300 hours!

✖ ✖ ✖

A store on New York's Upper West Side proclaims, "We Sell Everything!" "Can't be," Alvin thinks, and wanders in. Sure enough, the place is jam-packed with the most incredible items he's ever seen. He even stumbles across a stuffed rat! "What a terrific conversation piece," he thinks, and buys the rat.

As Alvin starts walking downtown with the rat under his arm, he notices two big rats following him. By 57th Street, there are 100 rats on his heels, and at 34th, the pack has grown to 500! Alvin picks up his pace, but no matter how fast he goes, he can't shake the rats and their number keeps growing!

By the time he reaches Battery Park, there are 7,000 rats behind him. Panic-stricken, Alvin breaks into a full gallop, heading for the river. The instant he reaches it, he hurls the stuffed rat into the water.

To his amazement, all 7,000 rats jump in after it and drown!

The next day, Alvin goes back to the shop and takes the owner aside. "Tell me," he says, "you wouldn't happen to have a stuffed lawyer for sale, would you?"

✴ ✴ ✴

My lawyer didn't want to marry his wife for her money. But there was no other way to get it!

✴ ✴ ✴

One lawyer I know has the soul of a sculptor. He carved out his career by first-class chiseling!

✸ ✸ ✸

All his life, a young lawyer named Bill has wanted to play at a fancy golf club in Westchester. One day, he finds himself passing by the club. On a whim, he goes in and asks if he can play a round. "Sorry, sir," the desk clerk tells him, "you have to be a member or a guest."

Bill is about to leave when he spots one of the most famous attorneys in the country sitting in the lounge. What the hell? Bill thinks. He straightens his tie, walks over, and introduces himself. "All my life, I've wanted a chance at this course. Would it be all right if I played just this once as your guest?"

The old lawyer looks him over. "Where do you live?" he asks.

"In Manhattan, on Sixty-third Street, between Madison and Park."

"What do you drive?"

"A Lincoln Towncar."

"How much do you bill an hour?"

"Two hundred."

The old lawyer sniffs disdainfully. Then he calls for the club's secretary, points to Bill, and says, "*Nine* holes."

✗ ✗ ✗

I offered to pay my lawyer what he's worth, but he won't work for nothing!

✗ ✗ ✗

Calvin is on the witness stand. Every time he answers, he says, "I think . . ."

The prosecutor finally gets fed up. "Don't think," he hollers, "just talk!"

"I can't," Calvin cries. "I'm not a lawyer!"

✗ ✗ ✗

What do you give a lawyer who marries a snake?

Towels marked "Hiss" and "Hiss"!

✖ ✖ ✖

The prosecutor is closing in on the defendant. "How can you swear that on the night in question you flew to Miami from Chicago? We have sworn affidavits proving the airport in Chicago was snowed-in, and Miami was closed due to heavy fog!"

The defendant's lawyer leaps to his feet and shouts, "That's our story and we're sticking to it!"

✖ ✖ ✖

My lawyer just put me back on my feet. His bill was so big, I had to sell my car!

✖ ✖ ✖

How can you tell when a lawyer's been using the computer? By the Wite-Out on the screen!

✗ ✗ ✗

When he was ten, my lawyer ran away with the circus. But the cops made him bring it back!

✗ ✗ ✗

A disheveled lawyer limps into a bar and orders a Scotch. When the bartender puts the drink before him, the lawyer starts to sob.

"What's wrong, pal?" the bartender asks.

"I just found out my mother died of a heart attack!"

"Gee, that's awful, but we all have to go sometime."

"It's not that," the lawyer said. "I wasted an hour chasing the ambulance!"

✖ ✖ ✖

Picture this. You're in a room with a frenzied shark, a famished lion and Lenny the lawyer. Luckily, you have a shotgun with two bullets. What do you do?

Shoot Lenny.

Twice!

✖ ✖ ✖

A doctor, a lawyer, and a minister find themselves adrift at sea in a lifeboat. They're out there for days. No food. No water. The situation is desperate. Suddenly, the lawyer stands up and says, "I'm going to swim to shore."

"You're nuts," the doctor says. "These are shark-infested waters. You'll never make it."

Nevertheless, the lawyer jumps in and, as the others watch, the sharks part, creating a free lane to shore.

"That's incredible!" the minister cries. "How could that happen?"

The doctor says, "Easy. Professional courtesy!"

✖ ✖ ✖

You know why cemeteries are beginning to bury lawyers 12 feet down? Because deep down they're good people!

✖ ✖ ✖

My lawyer is absolute proof of the theory of evolution. A barracuda with car keys!

✖ ✖ ✖

Lucille, Irene, and Monica are competing for a partnership in a large law firm. Suddenly, they all begin receiving $200 more a week in their paychecks, with no explanation. After a year, the senior partner calls them into his office.

"I was responsible for the surprise increase in your salaries," he announces. "Now, I'd like your views on it."

Lucille says, "Since the money was given freely and indicated to me that I was making progress in the firm, I considered it a gift. It's therefore rightfully mine. I'm sure any law partner would agree with me."

Next, Irene says, "I prize my integrity. Since I never knew what this money was for, I've been keeping it in an escrow account. I'm now prepared to return it to you. As I see things, my morality should be the ticket to a partnership for me."

Lastly, Monica speaks up. "From the moment I began receiving this extra money, I've been investing it in securities. I've more than doubled the amount, and I'm very willing to split it with you, as any fair-minded partner would."

Considering all three views, which woman became a partner in the firm?

Easy. The one with the best legs!

✵ ✵ ✵

A comic is hired to entertain at a lawyer's convention. At the end, he gets a big ovation. When it's over, he says, "Thank you. You can put your hands back in each other's pockets now!"

✖ ✖ ✖

Did you hear what happened when the trial lawyer's daughter asked her father for $50? The lawyer responded, "$40? What in the world do you need $30 for?"

✖ ✖ ✖

I know a lawyer who's a whiz at gardening. Where he walks, weeds won't grow!

✖ ✖ ✖

Two personal-injury lawyers, Hal and Vic,

are arguing. Hal yells, "I resent that innuendo. When the hell did you ever hear my honesty questioned?"

"Questioned?" Vic cries. "I never heard it mentioned!"

✳ ✳ ✳

There's a job opening in the country's most prestigious law firm, and it finally comes down to Ron and Phil.

Both graduated magna cum laude from law school. Both come from good families. Both are equally attractive and well-spoken. It's up to the senior partner to choose one, so he takes each aside and asks, "Why did you become a lawyer?" In seconds, he chooses Phil.

Baffled, Ron takes Phil aside. "I don't understand why I was rejected. When Mr. Armstrong asked me why I became a lawyer, I said that I had the greatest respect for the law, that I'd lay down my life for the Constitution, and that all I wanted was to do right by my clients. What in the world did you tell him?"

"I said I became a lawyer because of my hands," Ron replies.

"What do you mean, your hands?"

"Well, I took a look one day and there wasn't any money in either of them!"

✖ ✖ ✖

An honest man is a guy who never goes back on his word—without consulting his lawyer!

✖ ✖ ✖

Smith practiced law for 60 years. Finally, he drops dead. At the funeral, hundreds of people show up. A bystander turns to one and says, "What a turn-out."

The mourner says, "We were all clients of his."

"No kidding! All clients! And you all showed up to pay your respects!"

"Hell, no. We came to make sure he was dead!"

✖ ✖ ✖

My lawyer just bought himself a pool table and he doesn't even play. He just wanted six more pockets to go through!

✖ ✖ ✖

Siamese twins, Beau and Bob, are enlisting in the Army. The recruiting officer asks Beau, "What do you do for a living?"

"I'm a clown."

The officer puts a slash in the middle of the space for "Occupation." In the first half, he writes "Clown." Then he turns to the other twin.

"And what do you do?"

"I'm a lawyer," Bob says.

The recruiting officer thinks for a minute.

Then, in the second half of the box, he writes, "Ditto."

✖ ✖ ✖

I know a lawyer who had a real fright last night. He dreamed he was dead. The heat woke him up!

✖ ✖ ✖

An eccentric billionaire named Harrison dies. According to Harrison's will, his minister, doctor, and lawyer are each supposed to bury $50,000 in the coffin.

After the funeral, the executor of the will calls the three together to find out if they complied.

The minister says, "I buried everything but five thousand, which I gave to a needy parishioner with seven hungry kids."

"How about you?" the executor asks the doctor.

"I would have buried it all," the doctor says, "but my hospital needed a new dialysis machine, so I held back twenty thousand to buy one."

At this point, the lawyer shouts, "I can't believe you guys! Harrison made a simple request of us and you two welched! How can you live with yourselves?"

The executor beams. "You mean you fulfilled your obligation to the deceased, just as he requested?"

"Absolutely," the lawyer says. "I wrote him a check for the whole thing!"

✖ ✖ ✖

Even as a kid, my lawyer had to scrimp and scrape. He saved every cent he stole!

✖ ✖ ✖

A lawyer's head is full of trials, appeals, and reversals. Everything but convictions!

✖ ✖ ✖

A lawyer named Douglas bills a client for $3,500. A week later, the client mistakenly sends a check for $4,500, which puts Douglas in a moral predicament: Should he or shouldn't he tell his partners about the extra thousand?

✖ ✖ ✖

I'll say this for my lawyer. He was a great believer in hygiene. He did his best to take me to the cleaners!

✖ ✖ ✖

Johnny's kindergarten teacher phones his mother. "Mrs. Brown, I'm very distressed. Johnny breaks things and blames other children. He won't share his toys. He gobbles the cookies before anyone else can get them. Mrs.

Brown, if we don't nip this in the bud, Johnny's going to grow up to be a lawyer!"

✖ ✖ ✖

My lawyer's a lot like a nudist. You can't pin anything on either of them!

✖ ✖ ✖

New Jersey has the most toxic waste dumps, and California has the most lawyers. You know why? New Jersey had first choice!

✖ ✖ ✖

A lawyer named Morris and a rabbi are playing tennis in Forest Hills. Every time Morris misses a shot, he hollers, "I was that close, God damn it!" Finally, the rabbi says, "If you don't cut that out, God's going to unleash the wrath of the Old Testament on you!"

Things proceed quietly and Morris holds his tongue. Finally, he finds himself serving for the match. Morris takes a breath, raises his racket, and slams the ball into the fence. "God damn it, I was that close!" he cries.

Suddenly, the sky darkens, there's a roar of thunder, and a violent bolt of lightning pierces the heavens. When it's over, Morris discovers the rabbi lying dead on the ground.

From up above, a deep voice laments, "Damn! I was that close!"

✘ ✘ ✘

I can't say my lawyer picked pockets. He took them as they came!

✘ ✘ ✘

My lawyer's timing is good. But his two-timing is perfect!

✘ ✘ ✘

Did you hear about the lawyer who got a divorce? He's terribly upset. His wife got custody of their poodle, Patches, and the lawyer got visitation rights.

But Patches refuses to see him!

✘ ✘ ✘

Woodrow, the senior partner of a St. Louis law firm, suspects his staff goofs off when he leaves early, so one night, he sneaks back in. Sure enough, he spots all the associate lawyers watching a basketball game on cable in the conference room.

"I'll show them," Woodrow thinks, and deliberately triggers the security alarm.

To his amazement, nobody moves.

But about ten minutes later, a delivery boy shows up with two pizzas!

✘ ✘ ✘

To trust your lawyer, you need an open mind. A hole in the head!

✕ ✕ ✕

A guy rushes into a busy Chicago street and starts screaming, "Get me an ambulance!"
A cop comes over and says, "Are you hurt?"
"No. I just graduated from law school!"

✕ ✕ ✕

Epitaph for an attorney: "Motion denied!"

✕ ✕ ✕

My lawyer only wants the little things in life. A little real estate, a little gold, a little Swiss bank account . . .

✖ ✖ ✖

Did you hear about the old farmer in Nebraska who shot his wife dead?

He had some lawyer. Got him off scot-free.

"Have a heart, judge," the lawyer pleaded. "After all, my client's a widower!"

✖ ✖ ✖

A Beverly Hills lawyer named Marv suffers a severe heart attack. One of his partners pays a sick call and to cheer Marv up, he says, "The minute we heard you were sick, the partners voted to spend a minute in silent prayer for you."

Marv sits up a little higher in bed. "Really? That's wonderful! I had no idea you cared."

His partner nods and says, "See? And the vote passed five to four!"

✖ ✖ ✖

When it comes to working for his clients, my lawyer stops at nothing!

✖ ✖ ✖

My lawyer never worries ahead of time. He knows he can always double-cross a bridge when he comes to it!

✖ ✖ ✖

Remember when Clarence Thomas said, "I'd rather die than withdraw?" That's what probably got him in trouble in the first place!

✖ ✖ ✖

A philosophy student named Arthur wants to find the answer to the question "What equals two plus two?" First, he asks a mathematician, who goes on and on about the concept of a definite answer. Then, Arthur poses the question to a scientist, whose answer is equally confusing. Finally, Arthur approaches a lawyer. "What equals two plus two?" he asks. The lawyer smiles and says, "What would you like it to be?"

✖ ✖ ✖

One lawyer I know is a great believer in science. He's a human gimme-pig!

✖ ✖ ✖

Diogenes gets tired of searching for an honest man and decides to look for an honest lawyer instead. Several months later, he runs into his friend Caesar. "How's it going?" Ceasar asks.

"Pretty good," Diogenes says. "I've still got my lantern!"

✖ ✖ ✖

My lawyer is on a diet. He takes nothing but greens. Tens, twenties, fifties!

✖ ✖ ✖

Sing Sing is so overcrowded, a new release program goes into effect and the warden starts reviewing prisoners to see who's eligible.

The first one appears and the guard says, "Jones murdered his wife because she was late with dinner one night."

The warden frowns and says, "Release him."

The next prisoner steps forward. "Smith broke into six churches and cleaned out the poor box," the guard says.

The warden sighs. "Let him go."

The third prisoner steps forward. "Pomeroy here practiced law for fifteen years—"

The warden holds up his hand and says, "Two out of three ain't bad!"

✗ ✗ ✗

How are lawyers and sperm alike? Only one in a million ever does anything worthwhile!

✗ ✗ ✗

A young law-school graduate named Felix decides to practice law in the Navy. After he enlists, the first thing he does is hang up a sign in his office: NEVER GIVE UP THE SHIP. SELL IT!

✗ ✗ ✗

My lawyer was in a terrible accident the other day. In fact, he lost a toe. The ambulance backed up suddenly!

✗ ✗ ✗

Business is so slow, an Atlanta lawyer named Warren gives up his office and starts working from home. After a while, he decides to advertise in the paper. Naturally, he includes his home number.

At four in the morning, he gets a call from a guy named Moe in California.

"How can I help you?" Warren asks, groggily.

"You can't," Moe says. "*My* lawyer I can't reach! At least you answer the phone!"

✖ ✖ ✖

Have you heard about the ethical lawyer? Neither has anybody else!

✖ ✖ ✖

People don't realize it, but conscience is a valuable asset for a lawyer. The more he has, the more he gets for ignoring it!

✖ ✖ ✖

How are listening to a lawyer and eating Szechuan food alike? In both cases, you have to watch what you swallow!

✖ ✖ ✖

Jeremy is standing in front of St. Patrick's when he sees a funeral procession passing by. Behind the hearse, there's a man walking a tiger on a leash, and behind him, four hundred people are following.

Jeremy can't figure it out, so he walks up to the man with the tiger and says, "Forgive my curiosity, but what's this all about?"

"This is my lawyer's funeral. My tiger killed him."

Jeremy gets all excited and says, "How would you feel about loaning me your tiger?"

The man sticks his thumb over his shoulder and says, "Get in line!"

✖ ✖ ✖

Lawyers can be divided into three categories: honest, diligent, and the other 99 percent!

✖ ✖ ✖

The Stage Deli finally named a sandwich for a lawyer: cold shoulder and hot tongue!

✖ ✖ ✖

A drunken lawyer named Andy gets thrown out of a bar on Madison Avenue by the bartender. Twenty minutes later, the bartender spies him on a stool and hollers, "I told you not to come in here again!"

Andy looks up and says, "You mean you also work in this joint?"

✖ ✖ ✖

What's the difference between a lawyer and a prostitute? A prostitute stops screwing you after you're dead!

✖ ✖ ✖

A corporate lawyer named Mark is strolling through the jungle when he finds himself confronted by a wild male elephant. Mark turns to run, and spots a lion coming from that direction. Suddenly, he remembers he's got a pistol with him. Quickly, he pulls it out, only to find he's got just one bullet.

Without a second thought, Mark shoots the lion.

Which make sense.

A lawyer can always shoot the "bull!"

✖ ✖ ✖

I wouldn't say my lawyer inflates his hourly billing. Time flies—and *his* fights headwinds!

✖ ✖ ✖

Boy, was it cold yesterday!
How cold was it?
It was so cold, my lawyer kept his hands in his own pockets!

✖ ✖ ✖

The judge says, "How do you plead, innocent or guilty?"
Perry, the defense lawyer, says, "I respectfully request a postponement, Your Honor."
The judge waves his hand. "Just answer the question. How does your client plead, innocent or guilty?"
"To tell you the truth," Perry says, "we'd like to hear the evidence first!"

✖ ✖ ✖

Opportunities lie on every hand. And so do lawyers!

✖ ✖ ✖

Hiring a lawyer isn't a gamble—you've got half a chance with a gamble!

✖ ✖ ✖

After a day on the golf course in Scarsdale, a lawyer goes home and limps into the kitchen where his wife's making dinner.

"You look exhausted," she says. "How'd it go?"

"Terrible," he replies. "Henry dropped dead on the third hole."

"How awful!"

"Yeah," he says, rubbing his arm. "All day,

it was, hit the ball, drag Henry, hit the ball. . . ."

✖ ✖ ✖

What's the difference between a dead skunk in the road and a dead lawyer? You'll find skid marks in front of the skunk!

✖ ✖ ✖

You know how to light up your lawyer's eyes? Shine a flashlight in his ear!

✖ ✖ ✖

Jake and Harold are sitting in Central Park, watching the joggers go by. Harold says, "See that guy with gray hair? Take my word for it, he's a doctor. I can tell just by looking."

A few minutes later, he says, "That one with

the blue sweatpants owns an advertising agency."

Suddenly, the sound of a siren pierces the air as an ambulance races down Fifth Avenue. With that, a jogger leaves the path and tears out of the park.

"I suppose you know what he does, too," Jake sneers.

"Absolutely," Harold replies. "He's a lawyer!"

✖ ✖ ✖

Did you hear about the old lawyer who retired to a snake farm? He wanted to be among friends!

✖ ✖ ✖

A bunch of Chicago lawyers are sitting around the office playing poker. "I win," says Johnson, at which point Henderson throws down his cards. "That's it! I've had it! Johnson cheated!"

"How can you tell?" Phillips asks.
"Those aren't the cards I dealt him!"

❌ ❌ ❌

My lawyer's very democratic when it comes to representing clients. He doesn't care whose means he lives beyond!

❌ ❌ ❌

The wealthy emir of Abbydabby decides to hold a contest for lawyers. Whoever wins gets to handle all the emir's business. The day of the event, his estate is swamped with lawyers, all eager for his blessing.

"Gentlemen," the emir says, "please follow me." He leads them out to an enormous swimming pool that's filled with piranha. Then, he snaps his fingers. With that, a servant opens a door. A beautiful Arabian stallion rushes out and tumbles into the pool. In no time at all, the horse is nothing but bones.

The emir says, "Any man who can swim the length of this pool shall represent me in all my business and personal dealings."

Instantly, a lawyer named Carl pitches into the water. Furiously, he swims across the pool, hauls himself out and stands there panting.

"Bravo!" the emir shouts. "You have proven to me how much you want my business!"

"Actually, I just want one thing," Carl gasps.

"What's that?"

"The name of the bastard who shoved me in!"

✖ ✖ ✖

My lawyer is very flexible. He can put either hand in my pocket!

✖ ✖ ✖

Sometimes I get the feeling my lawyer is

doing the work of two: Bart and Homer Simpson!

✖ ✖ ✖

Someone mistakenly leaves the cages open in the reptile house at the Bronx Zoo and there are snakes slithering all over the place.

Frantically, the keeper tries everything, but he can't get them back in their cages. Finally, he phones the director of the zoo who says, "Quick! Get a lawyer!"

"A lawyer, why?"

"You need someone who speaks their language!"

✖ ✖ ✖

A New Orleans lawyer is offered a judgeship. "Thanks, but no thanks," he says. "I'd rather spend my time hurling the bull than ducking it!"

✘ ✘ ✘

What makes Saddam Hussein different from a divorce lawyer? Compared to a divorce lawyer, Hussein's behavior is reasonable!

✘ ✘ ✘

My lawyer believes in the cafeteria plan. Self-service only!

✘ ✘ ✘

What do you call it when you blow in a lawyer's ear?
A refill!

✘ ✘ ✘

Grant, a Park Avenue divorce lawyer, is defending a husband in court. When the wife takes the stand, Grant browbeats her so badly, she admits she once had an extra-marital affair and that she's only trying to exact revenge from her husband by claiming she needs $50,000-a-month support. When Grant's through, the woman has to be helped from the stand. Half an hour later, the judge rules in favor of the husband. Outside the courtroom, the husband says, "My God, did you have to be so rough on her?"

"What are you complaining about?" Grant says. "The end justified the meanness!"

✗ ✗ ✗

What a country! Only in America do they lock up the jury at night and let the lawyers go home!

✗ ✗ ✗

What's black and tan and looks good on an attorney? A Doberman pinscher!

✖ ✖ ✖

A lawyer visits his client in Attica on the eve of his execution.

"Even though you couldn't get me off, I know you really worked hard for me, Mr. Green," the condemned man says. "Do you have any final words for me?"

Green thinks for a minute. "Yeah," he says. "Don't sit down!"

✖ ✖ ✖

My lawyer had to become a lawyer because of his emotional make-up. He was too nervous to steal outright!

✖ ✖ ✖

I just sent my lawyer a little something for his birthday. Unfortunately, he wasn't home when it went off!

✖ ✖ ✖

Amy's pet parrot flies out an open window. Heartbroken, she rushes to the vet. "I've got just the thing for you," he says. "This gadget is a special remote buzzer. It makes a sound only parrots, buzzards, and deadly snakes can hear."

Amy buys it and goes home. Nervously, she sits down in the living room and presses the remote buzzer.

Ten minutes later, the parrot flies back in through the window. At the same time, Amy hears an awful racket in front of the house.

Curious, she opens the door. There, on her doorstep, are three buzzards and seven personal-injury lawyers!

✖ ✖ ✖

You know what a divorce lawyer is? A guy who gets richer by decrees!

✖ ✖ ✖

My lawyer makes anonymous donations to every single charity. He never signs the checks!

✖ ✖ ✖

It's the year 2020 and Simon walks into a brain shop. "What'll it cost me to get some new brains?"

The proprietor says, "Well, we charge three hundred dollars for an ounce of doctor's brains, six hundred for an ounce of brains from a Fortune Five Hundred CEO, and fifty thousand for an ounce of lawyer's brains."

Simon is flabbergasted. "I can't believe you charge so much for lawyer's brains!"

The proprietor says, "Do you know how

many lawyers have to die for me to collect an ounce of brains?"

✖ ✖ ✖

My lawyer doesn't believe in jogging on hills. The only thing he runs up is his bill!

✖ ✖ ✖

Betsy Ross once worked for a law firm. She made the loopholes!

✖ ✖ ✖

Three retired lawyers in Denver are talking about their old-age problems. Jacob says, "I always have trouble when I try to pee." Arnold says, "That's nothing. I have a terrible time trying to poop." Morris announces, "I don't have any trouble peeing or pooping. Every morning I pee at seven o'clock and poop at eight."

"That's wonderful," says Arnold.

"What's so wonderful? I don't wake up until ten!"

✖ ✖ ✖

I have a grand lawyer. Every time I consult him, it costs me a grand!

✖ ✖ ✖

My lawyer got a BMW for his wife. Now, that's what he calls a trade!

✖ ✖ ✖

One Sunday, a minister asks the town's most prominent lawyer to give the sermon. The lawyer, Wendell, decides the only way he can hold the congregation's attention is to speak about sex, so he does. Later, his wife says, "I'm sorry I couldn't hear you talk. What was your subject?"

Wendell flushes and lies. "I talked about sailing."

The next day, his wife runs into one of the parishioners who heard Wendell's sermon. "That was some discourse," the parishioner says. "Your husband is a true expert on the subject!"

"Really?" the wife says. "That surprises me. He's only done it three times. The first two, he got sick, and the third time his hat blew off!"

✗ ✗ ✗

Definition of a judge: a lawyer with something on the governor!

✗ ✗ ✗

A law-school graduate is being interviewed for a job. "Where do you see yourself in five years?" the senior partner asks.

The graduate looks at his watch and says, "Serving for the match!"

✖ ✖ ✖

"My fee comes to eleven thousand dollars," says Roger, a malpractice lawyer. His client gives a start and accidentally spills his coffee on Roger's desk.

"Got some tissues?" the client asks.

"Don't worry about it. The cleaning woman will take care of it," Roger says.

"Not for the coffee," the client says, "I'm going to be sick!"

✖ ✖ ✖

Small-town lawyers have it really difficult. It's hard to screw while everyone's watching!

✖ ✖ ✖

Did you hear about the florist who got his cards mixed up? To the new mother of quintuplets, he sent, "With sympathy." And to the funeral of a lawyer who went to heaven, he sent, "Congratulations on a remarkable achievement!"

✖ ✖ ✖

Successful lawyer: one who owns his own ambulance!

✖ ✖ ✖

I'll say this for my lawyer: He's got the courage of his connections!

✖ ✖ ✖

A lawyer named Jack gets divorced. A week later, Jack runs into an old friend. "I was shocked to hear about your divorce," the friend says. "What happened?"

"Would you put up with someone who lied, played around, and screwed your relatives?"

"Absolutely not."

"Well," says Jack, "neither would my wife!"

✖ ✖ ✖

I know a lawyer who got his client a suspended sentence. They hanged him!

✖ ✖ ✖

Lawyer: a guy you can count on to give his almost!

✖ ✖ ✖

A San Antonio lawyer driving a Mercedes makes a sudden stop at a red light, and a Honda behind him lightly bumps into his fender. Furious, the lawyer gets out, marches back to the Honda and hollers, "Moron! Monumental idiot! Incompetent jackass!"

The driver of the Honda puts his hand out the window and says, "Pleased to meet you. *My* name's Johnson!"

✖ ✖ ✖

Do you know why they call it practicing law? It takes time to learn how to get money from another guy's pocket without resorting to violence!

✖ ✖ ✖

Lawyers abide by the three R's: This is ours, that's ours, everything is ours!

✕ ✕ ✕

By the time my lawyer found out he had no talent for law, he was too successful to give it up!

✕ ✕ ✕

One Christmas, a corporate lawyer named Ronald goes to church for the first time in years.

After the sermon, the minister says, "I'd like to ask each parishioner to make a ten-percent donation so we can feed the poor over the holidays."

Ronald is so touched, he jumps up and cries, "Hell, I'll give a twentieth!"

✖ ✖ ✖

My lawyer's recovering from an unusual accident. He was struck by an honest thought!

✖ ✖ ✖

Two Wall Street lawyers have been partners for 30 years. Now, one of them is dying. In a faint voice, he says, "Sam, I've got to clear my mind before I go. I'm actually the father of your son! And five years ago, I began siphoning the firm's money into a numbered Swiss account. Can you ever forgive me?"

Sam takes his partner's hand and says, "Jerry, rest easy. I'm the one who poisoned your soup!"

✖ ✖ ✖

Finch, the head of a St. Louis law firm, is interviewing a young prospect who's looking for a job.

"Tell me, son, where'd you receive your legal education?"

"Yale."

"Fine. And by the way, what's your name?"

"Yonny Yames!"

❌ ❌ ❌

A new coffee shop opens up on Madison Avenue. The first morning, the owner puts out a sign that reads, KITCHEN OPEN.

By eleven, 14 lawyers signed up!

❌ ❌ ❌

What do you get with five lawyers at the bottom of the pool? Five air pockets!

❌ ❌ ❌

The old man's lawyer convinces him to leave his fortune to his niece, who just so happens to be engaged to the lawyer. After the funeral, everyone gathers for the reading of the will. In a solemn voice, the lawyer reads, "To my son, Andrew, I bequeath all my money and worldly goods."

"Hot dog!" says Andrew.

"Wait," the lawyer cautions. He withdraws a piece of paper from his pocket. "I have here a codicil to this will, in which Amanda Jones, the deceased's niece, is named sole benefactor."

"Damn!" cries Andrew.

"Oh, my!" swoons Amanda.

"Heh, heh!" chuckles the lawyer.

All of which proves the old maxim, out one heir, in the other!

✖ ✖ ✖

Cancel the cruise!

Why?

I just paid my legal fees, and beggars can't be cruisers!

✖ ✖ ✖

A lawyer and his wife go out for dinner. The waiter comes over and asks the wife, "May I take your order?"

"Yes. I'll have Dover sole, a Caesar salad, and boiled potatoes."

"What about the vegetable?" the waiter asks.

"He'll have the same!"

✖ ✖ ✖

Venal Law School's graduating class is posing for a picture. The photographer keeps moving them around. Finally, when he's got the shot he wants, he puts his finger on the shutter. "Okay," he tells them. "Say fees!"

✖ ✖ ✖

I know a personal-injury lawyer who's living

proof of reincarnation. Nobody can get that sleazy in just one lifetime!

✖ ✖ ✖

I'm having a hard time drowning my troubles. I can't get my lawyer near the water!

✖ ✖ ✖

A lawyer decides to pop the question. He takes his girl to the finest restaurant in the city and, after dinner, slips a huge diamond ring on her finger.

"Oh, Charles! I can't marry you. I just fell in love with a doctor!"

"Who is he?"

"Please, Charles. I don't want you to do anything drastic."

"What are you, crazy?" Charles says. "I just want to see what he'll give me for the ring!"

✖ ✖ ✖

I know a lawyer who's a real workaholic. His philosophy is "Dough or die!"

✖ ✖ ✖

I gave my lawyer a ticket for the rodeo. I wanted him to see the bull throwing people for a change!

✖ ✖ ✖

A group of lawyers go camping in the North Woods. One night, the temperature drops to freezing. They're huddled by the campfire when an old guy stumbles in. He's filthy and gasping for breath.

"My God!" one of the lawyers cries. "You look like you've been in Hell!"

"I have."

"Really? What's it like?"

The old guy looks around and says, "Pretty much like this. The lawyers are closest to the fire!"

✖ ✖ ✖

After 18 months, Harold's divorce is finally over. He calls his lawyer and says, "What are you going to charge me?"
"Are you sitting down?"
"Sitting? I'm kneeling!"

✖ ✖ ✖

You know what double jeopardy is? When your lawyer calls in his partner!

✖ ✖ ✖

On St. Patrick's Day, Kevin is strolling through Central Park when he spots a leprechaun. With one fell swoop, he captures it. "Now you have to grant me a wish," he says.

"True enough. What's your desire?"

Kevin pulls out a map of the world. "I want to rule everything from here to here!"

The leprechaun shakes his head. "I'd love to oblige, but I'm still in training and I don't think I have the power yet. Is there anything else I can do for you?"

Kevin thinks it over. Finally, he says, "I'll settle for the name of an honest lawyer."

The leprechaun sighs and says, "Let me look at that map again!"

✖ ✖ ✖

I can't believe what a big head my lawyer has. When the doctor tried to give him a local anesthetic, he demanded something imported!

✖ ✖ ✖

A Brooklyn lawyer named Ernie successfully

defends a major crime lord from charges of racketeering, murder, kidnaping, dealing drugs and selling arms.

As he's leaving the courtroom, an indignant old woman grabs him by the arm. "Young man, where are your scruples? Isn't there anyone too low for you to defend?"

"I don't know," Ernie says. "What have you done?"

✖ ✖ ✖

My lawyer respects old age—in a bottle!

✖ ✖ ✖

Did you hear about the lawyer who's with the FBI now? They nabbed him in L.A.!

✖ ✖ ✖

"The defendant was convicted of breaking into the vault of a Fifth Avenue hotel and stealing three hundred thousand dollars cash on May fifth," the judge says. "He's now accused of returning in July and taking one hundred and seventy-five thousand from the hotel's vault. Before I pronounce sentencing, does the defendant have anything to say?"

The defense lawyer rises and says, "Your honor, after his first burglary, my client learned that money can't buy happiness. This time, he was only trying to give it a second chance!"

✖ ✖ ✖

Practicing law is like driving a taxi. The meter keeps going even when you're standing still!

✖ ✖ ✖

Lawyer's Physiology

The footbone's connected to the ankle bone.
The ankle bone's connected to the shinbone.
The shinbone's connected to the kneebone.
The kneebone's connected to the thigh bone.
The thigh bone's connected to the backbone—
Wait a minute! There is no backbone!

✖ ✖ ✖

My lawyer's no dummy. He understands the
value of a dollar. These days, he wants his fee
in Swiss francs!

✖ ✖ ✖

A corporate lawyer and Mother Teresa get stranded in the desert. Two weeks later, a rescue plane lands. The pilot finds Mother Teresa lying dead, while the lawyer is calmly resting with his hands under his head.

"This is awful," the pilot says. "Mother Teresa dead!"

"Yeah."

"Tell me, how come you survived and she didn't?"

The lawyer shrugs. "She never found the water hole!"

✖ ✖ ✖

You know the difference between a football and a lawyer? The most you can get for kicking a football between the uprights is three points!

✖ ✖ ✖

I met my lawyer for lunch and made a

Freudian slip. Instead of saying, "Please pass the salt," I said, "You son of a bitch, you're robbing me blind!"

✖ ✖ ✖

Do you know how to save five drowning lawyers?
No?
Good!

✖ ✖ ✖

A young woman stops a personal-injury lawyer on the street and says, "Would you like to become a Jehovah's Witness?"
The lawyer shakes his head. "Sorry, I can't. I didn't see the accident!"

✖ ✖ ✖

My lawyer stands on his record. He has to. He's scared stiff someone'll read it!

✖ ✖ ✖

A Frenchman, a Swiss, an American dentist and an American lawyer are traveling cross-country in the same compartment on an Amtrak train. After a while, the Frenchman opens a 100-year-old bottle of wine, takes a sip, and tosses it out the window.

"What a terrible waste," the American dentist says.

The Frenchman smiles. "Not so. France will never run out of wine."

Then, the Swiss opens a briefcase full of wristwatches. He puts on one worth $50,000 and, two minutes later, throws it out the window. Before the dentist can say a word, the Swiss laughs and says, "Switzerland will never be at a loss for timepieces."

The American dentist thinks for a moment. Then he stands up, seizes the American lawyer and hurls him out the window!

✖ ✖ ✖

A TV repairman gets called to a lawyer's house. In ten minutes, he's got the VCR working perfectly and hands the lawyer a bill for $1,000.

The lawyer becomes irate. "My hourly rate is high, but nothing like this!"

"Neither was mine when *I* practiced law!"

✖ ✖ ✖

Lawyers don't snore in their sleep. They cackle!

✖ ✖ ✖

My lawyer's a whiz at poker, but he never wins at the dog track. They won't let him shuffle the greyhounds!

✳ ✳ ✳

Did you hear about the divorce lawyer who died and caused a lot of hardship? He left a wife, two kids, and three judges without support!

✳ ✳ ✳

Two lawyers, Frank and Harry, meet for a drink. Frank says, "You know what happened? An angel was sent down to compile the names of all the dishonest lawyers on earth. Six months later, he dragged himself back to Heaven, exhausted. 'Believe me,' he told God, 'it'd be easier if I just made note of all the *honest* lawyers on earth. In fact, I could do that over the weekend.' God said, 'Fine.' Come Monday morning, the angel turned in his list and God said, 'That's terrific. Now I think you should send all the lawyers on this list a note of congratulations.'"

Frank pauses and sips his Scotch. Then he

says, "There was a postscript to the angel's note. You know what it was?"

Harry says, "No."

"Aha! So you didn't get one either!"

✖ ✖ ✖

A pickpocket is being sentenced in Salt Lake City. The judge says, "Three hundred dollars or thirty days in jail."

The pickpocket's lawyer leans over and whispers in his ear, "Take the money!"

✖ ✖ ✖

I know a lawyer who's got such a bad memory, whenever he knocks on wood, he hollers, "Come in!"

✖ ✖ ✖

My lawyer and I have a give-and-take relationship. I give and he takes!

✖ ✖ ✖

Classified papers are being stolen left and right from the Justice Department. One morning, two legal secretaries are discussing the situation. "From now on, my boss is going to commit things to memory," says Jane.

"That's perfect," Rebecca says. "No one's ever found anything there yet!"

✖ ✖ ✖

I'd like to take the afternoon off for my lawyer's funeral. But he's as healthy as a horse!

✖ ✖ ✖

The Lawyers'
Daily Appointment Book

9:00AM—Running in place.
10:00AM—Chewing the fat.
11:00AM—Beating around the bush.
12:00 Noon—Lunch.
2:00PM—Dragging his feet.
3:00PM—Shooting the breeze.
4:00PM—Passing the buck.
5:00PM—Cooling his heels.

✖ ✖ ✖

I've got good news and bad news. The bad news is, the world's going to end on Friday. The good news is, there'll be no more lawyers!

✖ ✖ ✖

Jerry, a public defender, is at the Suffolk County jail, interviewing his client, an old vagrant. "I'll do my best to defend you, but you've got to tell me the truth. Did you do it?"

The vagrant hangs his head. "Yeah. I stole four cans of Perrier."

"Ha!" cries Jerry, with glee. "They can't make a case out of that!"

✖ ✖ ✖

What do you call ten lawyers lined up ear to ear?

A wind tunnel!

✖ ✖ ✖

Know why you never see lawyers on the beach?

The cats keep covering them up with sand!

✗ ✗ ✗

A wealthy Chicago banker is wiped out by his divorce and decides to breed pit bulls. One day, a friend drops by. "Sell any pups yet?" he asks.

"No, but things are great!" the banker says.

"Oh? How so?"

"My wife's lawyer walked by the other day and Killer bit him four times!"

✗ ✗ ✗

What's the thinnest book ever published? *The Lawyer's Book of Ethics!*

✗ ✗ ✗

A Connecticut state trooper is testifying in a drunk-driving case. The defense attorney says, "Officer Jackson, you say the defendant kept fumbling around in the glove com-

LAWYERS FROM HELL JOKE BOOK

partment for his registration. What time was it?"

"Midnight."

"It was dark, then?"

"Yes."

"And you admit the overhead light was broken?"

"Yes."

"Then how does my client's fumbling prove he was drunk?"

"We were in my squad car!"

✗ ✗ ✗

Hear about the lawyer who had a close call with death? He was revived at the last minute. Somebody up there didn't like him!

✗ ✗ ✗

A lawyer complains to his partner, "I feel awful today. I'm sluggish and wheezy."

"Whenever I feel like that," his partner says, "I make love to my wife, Fran. Snaps me right out of it."

The first lawyer shrugs and says, "Okay. Is Fran free for lunch?"

✖ ✖ ✖

What do you call a lawyer with an I.Q. of 70?

Your Honor!

✖ ✖ ✖

An investment lawyer is helping his nine-year-old son with his English homework.

"Dad, what comes after a sentence?"

"An appeal!"

✖ ✖ ✖

What's the difference between your lawyer and a trampoline? You're not supposed to jump on a trampoline with your shoes on!

✖ ✖ ✖

A Houston lawyer gets a frantic call from his wife. "Little Jennifer just swallowed a penny, and when I smacked her on the back, she spit out two nickels. What should I do?"

"Start feeding her dimes!"

✖ ✖ ✖

It's her first day on the job with the law firm Allen, Allen, and Allen, and the receptionist is very nervous. When she answers the first call, a man says, "Put me through to Sam Allen, please."

"One moment, sir."

Two minutes later, she gets back on the line and says, "I'm sorry, sir, but he's dead!"

"Oh, dear, I'm so embarrassed."

"You? *I* paged him!"

✖ ✖ ✖

My lawyer believes in principles. It's the practicing he can't stand!

✖ ✖ ✖

Why should you always have a lawyer at a picnic?
Because even flies won't land on one!

✖ ✖ ✖

A New York woman walking up the steps of the courthouse in Foley Square is muttering to herself, "I hate lawyers! I'll never marry another one again. In fact, if I ever do remarry, it'll be to someone I can trust, like a pediatrician."

A woman coming down the steps overhears her and says, "Wait here. There'll be one available in fifteen minutes!"

✖ ✖ ✖

Two lions are walking in the jungle. Suddenly, one of them rushes to the side of the road and starts devouring elephant droppings. The other lion cries, "What the hell are you doing?"

"Sorry. I just ate a lawyer and I had to get the taste out of my mouth!"

✖ ✖ ✖

What has four legs and chases Katz?
Mrs. Katz and her lawyer!

✖ ✖ ✖

Jim, Jack, and Jeff are walking on Malibu Beach when they stumble on a lamp with a genie in it. Naturally, he agrees to grant each one a wish.

Jim says, "I wish I were as handsome as Tom Selleck."

The genie snaps his fingers and says, "*Poof.* You're gorgeous."

Jack says, "I wish I were as talented as Robert DeNiro."

The genie yawns, waves his hand and says, "You're Oscar material."

Finally, Jeff says, "I wish I were a thousand times wealthier."

The genie reaches into his pocket, pulls out a piece of paper and hands it to Jeff. "Congratulations. Here's your law degree!"

✕ ✕ ✕

A Los Angeles lawyer has a terrible memory. To remind him of a case he's about to try, his partner leaves a note on his desk that reads, "Fred—embezzler."

The next morning, the partner finds a note

on his desk that says, "Who are you to criticize?"

✖ ✖ ✖

My lawyer's son got his intelligence from his dad. My lawyer's wife still has hers!

✖ ✖ ✖

George, a lawyer for a huge oil company, dies and goes to Heaven. The angel on duty explains, "You're free to go anywhere except to the clouds over there marked, 'Reserved.' "

"Why? Who's that for?"

"People of integrity," the angel says.

"Hey, I'm a person of integrity! I phoned the *Wall Street Journal* and told them my company lied about its efforts to protect the environment. I also cited six cases where my bosses smeared other employees who blew the whistle on them. Don't you have any of that on record?"

The angel looks perplexed. "Why, no. When did you do it?"

George looks at his watch and says, "Thirty seconds ago!"

✖ ✖ ✖

How are lawyer's like mushrooms? They both thrive in dark places with lots of crap!

✖ ✖ ✖

If I had but one life to give for my country, it would be my lawyer's!

✖ ✖ ✖

How many lawyers does it take to change a lightbulb?

It depends. Are you talking hourly rate or contingency fee?

✖ ✖ ✖

A divorce lawyer calls his client. "Harry, I just finished negotiating with your wife's lawyer."

"And?"

"As we left it, the party hereunder referred to in the second part, being of meagre means and manner of income, it was agreed said party would have claim to said domicile, all means of transportation attached thereto, in addition to all monetary assets."

Harry scratches his head. "I don't get any of that."

"That's right!"

✖ ✖ ✖

What does a lawyer do after he dies?
Lie. Still!

✖ ✖ ✖

I asked my lawyer how he wants to be remembered and he said, "In the emir of Kuwait's will!"

✖ ✖ ✖

Why can't lawyers go scuba diving?
They leave oil slicks!

✖ ✖ ✖

After a Park Avenue cocktail party, three couples get killed in a collision with a bus. Now, they're being questioned by St. Peter.

"Why should I let you enter?" he asks Barney, the druggist.

"Well, I took good care of my kids."

"Yes, but you loved liquor so much you drank like a fish and even married a woman named Sherry. Go to Hell!"

"Why should I let *you* in?" St. Peter asks Phil, the mechanic.

"I never caroused and I worked hard all my life," Phil says.

"True, but you were a glutton. In fact, you loved food so much, you married a woman named Sweet Sue. No admittance!"

Just as St. Peter turns to Charlie, the lawyer, Charlie grabs his wife and says, "Let's go, Penny, we're outta here!"

✖ ✖ ✖

A lawyer is someone who looks at a book a foot thick and calls it a "brief."

✖ ✖ ✖

Did you hear about the restaurant for Japanese lawyers that opened the other day? It's called So-Sumi!

✖ ✖ ✖

A terrible predicament arises when an old Texas lawyer dies. He was such a bastard, no one wants to give the eulogy. Finally, Wanda, his secretary of 25 years, agrees to get up and speak. Wanda walks to the front of the funeral parlor, faces the assembled crowd, and says, "His partner was worse!"

✖ ✖ ✖

I know a lawyer and his wife who have the perfect marriage. They're both in love with the same man!

✖ ✖ ✖

An entertainment lawyer named Marty drops dead the same time the Pope does. After the two pass through the Pearly Gates, St. Peter escorts Marty to a magnificent suite furnished with antiques. Then, he walks the Pope down the hall to a small room with a bare wooden floor, a tiny bed, one chair and a small table.

"You'll be staying here," St. Peter says.

With tears in his eyes, the Pope says, "I've been doing God's work on earth for thirty-five years. I've lived a humble life, thinking only of my mission. I don't want to appear crass, but how come I get this cell and Marty gets that incredible suite?"

"Popes we got by the dozen," St. Peter says. "Marty is our first entertainment lawyer!"

✖ ✖ ✖

My lawyer is a very good listener. He doesn't miss a word when money talks!

✖ ✖ ✖

I know a personal-injury lawyer who's so fast on his feet, he gets to the hospital before the ambulance!

✖ ✖ ✖

Two lawyers, Ralph and Sid, are in Times Square late one night when a guy pulls a gun on them. "Move into the alley and give me your money," he snarls.

As the lawyers start walking, Ralph feels Sid's hand in his jacket pocket. "What're you doing?" he whispers.

"Quick, take it!"

"What is it?"

"The fifty I owe you!"

✖ ✖ ✖

Lawyers. It's incredible how they can squander your money puttin' on the writs!

✖ ✖ ✖

A lawyer rushes into a San Francisco courtroom, out of breath. "Sorry I'm late, Your

Honor. My wife fainted and keeled over the sink while I was shaving."

"Good grief!" says the judge. "What did you do?"

"I finished in the tub!"

✖ ✖ ✖

What do you get when you cross a lawyer with a Mafioso?

A hit-man who misses!

✖ ✖ ✖

There are these two lawyers, Woody and Vic. Woody never misses church; he even prays twice a day. Vic, on the other hand, is an atheist. One day, they find themselves arguing a case against each other in court. Every time Woody rises to make an objection, he mumbles, "Lord, make the judge sustain me." Fifty times, he objects, and fifty times, he's overruled. In the end, he loses the case.

Bright and early the next day, Woody's kneeling in church. "Lord," he says sadly, "I've been pious my entire life. I observe all your laws. I pray constantly. Why didn't you have the judge sustain any of my objections during the trial? And how in the world could you let Vic win the case? He's a non-believer."

From a distance, a voice booms, "*He* doesn't pester the hell out of me!"

✖ ✖ ✖

My lawyer, Irv, gave up the bar to join Barnum & Bailey's Circus.

Really?

Yeah, he became a contortionist.

How come?

Now, he's *supposed* to make an "ess" out of himself!

✖ ✖ ✖

Personal-injury lawyers are really something when it comes to commercials. I saw one that goes:

"Had an accident? We couldn't be happier! Dial 1-800-MAIMED.

If you've lost a limb, press one now.

If your doctor has removed a vital organ during a routine examination, press two now.

If you're in a coma, please hold!"

> *lost an arm 2 million $*
> *lost a finger a million $*

✕ ✕ ✕

maybe you'll be the next lucky one.

Did you hear about the lawyer who found a way to take it with him?

Traveler's checks!

✕ ✕ ✕

How many lawyers does it take to change a lightbulb? Six. One to change the bulb, and five to file the environmental impact report!

✖ ✖ ✖

A minister, a boxer, and a lawyer named Fritz are asked, "What would you do if an ax murderer broke into your house and the only way you could save yourself was by letting him hack up your wife?"

The minister says, "I'd engage him in prayer and hope the Lord would intervene."

The boxer says, "I'd keep him talking, get close to him and, the first chance I got, I'd deliver a smashing right to his jaw."

Fritz the lawyer scratches his head and says, "Wait a minute. I don't see the problem here!"

✖ ✖ ✖

What do you call ten lawyers standing in a circle?

A dope ring!

✖ ✖ ✖

Divorce lawyer: "Before I take your case, Mrs. Henderson, are you sure you want to do this?"

"Absolutely. We're incompatible."

"How so?"

"I'm a Leo and he's a schmuck!"

✗ ✗ ✗

A woman rushes up the steps of the New Jersey State Courthouse. A guard is sitting by the door. Breathlessly, she asks, "Are there any criminal lawyers here?"

The guard says, "Yeah, but we can't prove it!"

✗ ✗ ✗

A group of cannibals in New Guinea is throwing a barbecue to raise funds for the community. The blackboard reads:

HONEYED TOURIST—$7.50

SWEET-AND-SOUR PHOTO-JOURNALIST—$10.50

LEMON-LIME LAWYER—$85.00

A guest takes one of the cannibals aside and says, "Why are you charging so much for the lemon-lime lawyer? It's way out of proportion with the other dishes."

"Hey," the cannibal says, "you know what it takes to clean one of them?"

✖ ✖ ✖

My lawyer went swimming on a deserted beach and almost drowned. Lucky for him he's two-faced. He gave himself mouth-to-mouth resuscitation!

✖ ✖ ✖

Did you know that one out of ten in Washington is a lawyer? The other nine are humans!

✖ ✖ ✖

Now it can be told. You know why we won the Gulf War so quickly? We had a special detail of lawyers at the front. And if it's one thing lawyers know, it's how to charge!

✖ ✖ ✖

Did you hear about the lawyer who had to be confined to a mental institution? He kept hearing honest invoices!

✖ ✖ ✖

Definition of gross ignorance: 144 lawyers!

✖ ✖ ✖

A lawyer's wife phones him at the office. "How are things going, Jim?"

"Great! The verdict just came in on that insider-trading case and my client was acquitted. The Bar Association just named me Lawyer of the Year, and I've been asked to plead before the Supreme Court next month!"

His wife yawns and says, "Sorry, honey. I didn't know you had company!"

✖ ✖ ✖

I know a lawyer who met his wife in a travel agency. She was looking for the last resort!

✖ ✖ ✖

A young female lawyer named Emily sews up her first merger. She's so excited, she can't think straight, so Emily calls in a male colleague. "Jones just offered me five hundred thousand dollars less five-and-a-quarter percent. How much should I take off for him?"

Her colleague thinks and says, "Everything but your watch!"

✖ ✖ ✖

Santa Claus, the Easter Bunny, and a cheap lawyer are sitting at a table. There's a glass of red wine on the table. Which of the three can't drink it?

The cheap lawyer, of course.

Everyone knows there is no such thing!

✖ ✖ ✖

An inept plastic surgeon falls asleep on the beach in Monaco. When he wakes up, he sees a fin in the water, gliding to shore. The plastic surgeon leaps to his feet, points to the fin and screams, "Lawyer! Lawyer!"

✖ ✖ ✖

A Washington lawyer dies and goes to heaven. When St. Peter appears, the lawyer becomes irate. "Why am I dead? I'm only thirty-six years old!"

St. Peter says, "Really? From your hourly billings, we figured you were at least a hundred and ten!"

✖ ✖ ✖

Why did God make snakes before lawyers? For the practice!

✖ ✖ ✖

No one can say my lawyer doesn't have any expertise.

He specializes in banking!

✖ ✖ ✖

My lawyer is so full of himself. He made an airline reservation the other day and when the clerk asked, "What class?" my lawyer said, "Upper!"

✖ ✖ ✖

A senator, a lawyer, and a minister are stranded in the woods. Suddenly, they come upon a farmhouse. The farmer says, "You can all stay the night, but I only have room in the house for two. One of you will have to sleep in the barn."

"I'll go," the minister says, and everyone retires.

An hour later, there's a knock on the farmer's door. It's the minister. "I'm afraid I can't sleep with the pigs after all," he says. "It's against my religious beliefs."

"I'll do it," the senator says, and he goes out to the barn. An hour later, there's another knock on the farmer's door. "Sleeping with pigs simply goes against my ethics," the senator says.

"All right, *I'll* do it," says the lawyer, and he treks out to the barn.

Ten minutes later, there's a knock on the door.

It's the pigs!

✖ ✖ ✖

Why won't your lawyer ever get pickled?
He can't fit his head in the jar!

✖ ✖ ✖

Many lawyers have offices in New York City's Woolworth Building. Which makes sense. They're constantly nickel-and-diming each other to death!

✖ ✖ ✖

Did you hear about the guy who looked high and low for a lawyer and couldn't find one? He didn't look low enough!

✖ ✖ ✖

A 95-year-old lawyer named Abe is having an affair with his young secretary. When his wife finds out, she surprises the couple in bed.

Whipping out a gun, she forces Abe to jump out the window.

"Why in the world did you do that?" her lawyer asks later.

"Because if Abe can screw at ninety-five, he can fly!"

✖ ✖ ✖

Lawyers really get a bad rap. After all, their clients usually have divided opinions about them. Half despise them; the other half detest them!

✖ ✖ ✖

A middle-aged lawyer named Harvey is chatting with his wife. "Do you believe in reincarnation?" he asks.

"No. Do you?"

"Yes," Harvey says. "And I can't decide if I'd rather be successful or handsome in my next life."

"What's the difference?" his wife says. "A change is a change!"

❌ ❌ ❌

How can you tell when a lawyer's lying?
His lips are moving!

❌ ❌ ❌

What's the difference between an attorney and the scum of the earth? . . . Well?
I'm thinking! I'm thinking!

❌ ❌ ❌

An environmental lawyer is cross-examining a state official in a huge oil-spill case.

"Tell me, sir, weren't you given one hundred thousand dollars by Screwyou Oil to fix this case?"

The witness stares into space, so the lawyer repeats the question.

Still, the witness remains silent.

Finally, the judge gets annoyed. "Mr. Profitt, I instruct you to answer counsel's question!"

"Sorry, Your Honor. I thought he was talking to you!"

✖ ✖ ✖

My lawyer has TGIF printed on the front of his shoes. Toes Go In Front!

✖ ✖ ✖

Bernard is trying his first case. His client is accused of stealing $300 from a nursery, plus half a dozen philodendron plants.

"Judge, have pity on him," Bernard pleads. "He needed the money to feed his family."

"I can understand that, but what about the philodendrons?"

"He has lousy luck with English ivy!"

✖ ✖ ✖

Definition of a personal injury lawyer: a guy who makes a mountain out of a molehill, and then sells climbing boots!

✖ ✖ ✖

A woman married to a lawyer gives him a cemetery plot for Christmas. The next year, she doesn't give him anything.

"Why no gift?" he asks.

"You didn't use last year's yet!"

✖ ✖ ✖

A lawyer named Charles and his wife are invited to a costume party.

"I can't decide how to dress," Charles says.

"Wear something that reflects your occupation," his wife says. "Loafers and a slicker!"

✖ ✖ ✖

My lawyer invested $100,000 in precious metals.

He bought a Ferrari!

✖ ✖ ✖

How many lawyers does it take to eat a dead skunk in the middle of the road?

Two. You need one to detour the traffic!

✖ ✖ ✖

My lawyer's a perfectionist. He takes great pains—and passes them on!

✖ ✖ ✖

NASA's chief counsel is trying to come up with some way to revitalize the space program. One night, it comes to him. He seizes the phone and dials the director. "I've got it! We'll send a man to the sun!"

The director sighs. "That's impossible. He'll be incinerated."

"No, you don't understand," the counsel cries. "We'll send him at night!"

✖ ✖ ✖

A law student's wife gets fed up one night. "Hank, I'm terribly embarrassed about how we live. Your mother pays our rent. My mother buys all our food. You should be ashamed!"

"You're right, honey. So far, your grandparents don't pay for a thing!"

✖ ✖ ✖

My lawyer knows what it takes to build a wardrobe. He's got dozens of suits!

✖ ✖ ✖

Hear about the Chicago lawyer who planned a surprise trip for his wife? He sent her a wire from Rio!

✖ ✖ ✖

A doctor, an architect, and a lawyer find themselves at the Pearly Gates. St. Peter comes out and says, "We're all booked up. I only have room for one of you and it will have to be the one whose profession was mentioned first in the Bible."

The doctor steps forward. "I'm your man. After all, God took a rib from Adam to make Eve. Clearly, that was a medical procedure."

"Wait," says the architect. "Adam and Eve came *after* the earth was created. Beforehand, there was nothing but chaos. Obviously, an architect supplied the blueprints to create the world as we know it."

Suddenly, the lawyer shoulders his way forward and cries, "Just a minute. Who the hell do you think created the chaos?!"

✳ ✳ ✳

There's only one way to make your lawyer laugh on Friday. Tell him a joke on Monday!

✳ ✳ ✳

Every day when the coffee cart stops by the office, a corporate lawyer named Sal buys a cheese danish and coffee, and every day, he tells the cart owner, "I'll pay you next week."

Finally, Sal's secretary says, "You never pay the guy. Doesn't that embarrass you?"

"Hell, no. He thinks I'm buying you breakfast!"

✗ ✗ ✗

Most people go through periods in their lives. Lawyers go through dollar signs!

✗ ✗ ✗

How can you tell a reputable jeweler from a lawyer?

A reputable jeweler will back your watch. A lawyer makes you watch your back!

✗ ✗ ✗

Fred and Barney are sharing a cell in Alcatraz. Fred sighs. Then he mutters, "Son of a bitch!" Two minutes later, he mumbles, "Miserable conniving bastard!"

At which point, Barney says, "I thought we agreed not to discuss lawyers anymore!"

✖ ✖ ✖

The Pope and a real-estate lawyer land at La Guardia Airport during a taxi strike. The lawyer says, "I'd be happy to give you a lift in my Mercedes, Your Holiness."

"Thank you, my son. I accept your offer, but I insist on driving, to show my appreciation." So the two of them take off for Manhattan with the Pope behind the wheel, the lawyer in the back seat.

Unaccustomed to driving, it's not long before the Pope is tearing down the Grand Central Parkway at 80 miles an hour. Within minutes, a cop pulls him over. Naturally, the cop recognizes the Pope and decides to call in and check with his sergeant at the station house.

"This guy I just stopped is pretty important. I'm not sure I should give him a ticket."

"Who is it, the mayor?" the sergeant asks.

"No, bigger than the mayor."

"You mean the governor?"

"No," the cop says, "much bigger."

"Don't tell me, the President!"

"No, bigger."

"For cryin' out loud, who the hell is it?" the sergeant cries.

"I don't know, but he's got the Pope chauffeuring him around!"

✖ ✖ ✖

How many lawyers does it take to screw in a lightbulb?

Just one. Don't you know the world revolves around *him*?

✖ ✖ ✖

Jerome and Alice are getting a divorce. Je-

same

rome runs a notice in the paper saying, "Not responsible for my wife's debts."

The next day, Alice's lawyer runs an ad below it that says, "We'll see!"

in the same paper

✖ ✖ ✖

I knew a lawyer who had the Midas touch. Everything he touched turned into a muffler!

✖ ✖ ✖

They're the only two lawyers in town and their rivalry is fierce. When Marvin buys a new gadget for his limo, he immediately picks up his cellular and calls Frank's car phone. "Hi, pal. Just thought I'd say hello. But, wait! I've got to pull over. There's something coming in over my fax!"

Frank says, "That's all right. It'll give me a chance to turn off my jacuzzi!"

✗ ✗ ✗

Josh meets his long-lost buddy Ernie on the street. "How come you got a cast on your arm?" Josh asks.

"I broke it."

"How?"

"Car accident, last spring."

"You broke your arm last spring and you're still in a cast?" Josh says.

"Yeah. My lawyer tells me I'm not healed yet!"

✗ ✗ ✗

The Bar Association can't decide where to hold its annual convention, but they've narrowed it down to two sites for sentimental reasons: Fort Knox and Sioux City!

How would that look?

✗ ✗ ✗

"Your Honor, I want to bring to your attention how unfair it is for my client to be accused of theft. He arrived in New York City a week ago and barely knows his way around. What's more, he only speaks a few words of English."

The judge looks at the defendant and says, "How much English can you speak?"

The defendant looks up and says, "Give me your wallet!"

✖ ✖ ✖

Two lawyers, Howard and Albert, charter a small passenger plane to fly to New York. Just outside LaGuardia Airport, the pilot drops dead. "Don't worry," cries Howard, "I think I can land this baby!" He seizes the controls and heads for the runway. Just as the wheels touch down, he throws the engine in reverse, jams on the brakes, and brings the plane to a violent stop.

Howard wipes his brow and says, "Brother, what a short runway!"

Albert looks side to side and says, "Yeah—but look how *wide* it is!"

✳ ✳ ✳

In a San Francisco courthouse, the plaintiff's lawyer is passionately arguing his case. Suddenly, the building starts shaking. It's an earthquake!

"See?" the defendant's lawyer cries. "Heaven agrees with me!"

The plaintiff's lawyer shouts, "Objection, Your Honor! Earthquakes originate ~~under-ground~~!" *below*

✳ ✳ ✳

Nat is accused of stealing a suit of clothes from a posh Fifth Avenue men's store. The judge studies him and says, "Wait a minute. Weren't you up before me ~~two months~~ ago for precisely the same reason, stealing a suit of clothes? I ought to throw the book at you."

about a year

Nat's lawyer stands up. "Your Honor, have mercy. They don't make things like they used to!"

❌ ❌ ❌

A lawyer named Elliot is filling out a job application at a New York State agency. Next to "Have you ever been arrested?" he writes, "No."

Only those who answer "yes" are supposed to answer the next question, which is "Why?"

But without thinking, Elliot jots down, "Too smart!"

❌ ❌ ❌

A lawyer's wife dies. At the cemetery, people are appalled to see that the tombstone reads, "Here lies Phyllis, wife of Murray, L.L.D., Wills, Divorce, Malpractice."

Suddenly, Murray bursts into tears. His

brother says, "You *should* cry, pulling a stunt like this!"

Through his tears, Murray croaks, "You don't understand. They left out the phone number!"

✖ ✖ ✖

Freddie walks into a bar in New Orleans with his pit bull, Spot. "You serve lawyers?" he asks the bartender.

"Sure do."

"Good. I'll have a Scotch, and Spot here'll have a litigator!"

✖ ✖ ✖

An investment lawyer named Sid retires to a secluded farm on a lake in Vermont. Two months later, he visits the doctor. "I don't know what's wrong," he complains, "but since my wife and I have been up here, our sex life has totally collapsed."

"Too bad. Tell me, when are *you* most in the mood?"

"Well," says Sid, "about ten in the morning, when I'm jogging around the lake. I immediately run home, but by the time I get there, I'm breathless and totally out of energy."

The doctor says, "From now on, take a shotgun with you and when the mood strikes, fire the gun. That'll be a signal for your wife to rush out and join you, and you can cohabitate near the lake."

"Great idea!" Sid says, and hurries home.

Two weeks later, he calls the doctor. "I can't thank you enough. My sex life is absolutely tremendous since my wife and I put your plan into action."

"Glad to hear it," the doctor says.

A year passes, and one day the doctor spots Sid in town. "How's the little woman?" he asks.

Sid wipes away a tear. "Dead."

"My goodness, what happened?"

"She ran herself to death during hunting season!"

✖ ✖ ✖

Two Twin Cities lawyers are arguing about the authenticity of the Bible. The one from Minneapolis says, "We have such a problem taking the Bible as fact, my city doesn't even *allow* the preaching of the New Testament."

The St. Paul lawyer says, "That's amazing! How come?"

"Because all the New Testament talks about is St. Paul. You never see a word about Minneapolis!"

✖ ✖ ✖

Marvin is the slimiest lawyer in Jersey City. Nevertheless, when he suffers a heart attack and falls into a coma, his secretary Jean calls an ambulance.

The emergency crew gets Marvin on a gurney and hoists him into the ambulance. Just as they're pulling out, Jean reluctantly decides, "I guess I'd better go with him," and climbs in, too.

The ambulance doesn't get two blocks away before it hits a huge pothole. The gurney gives a violent jerk and, miraculously,

Marvin comes out of his coma. Angrily, he glares at Jean. "What the hell are you doing *here*?" he hollers. "Who's going to answer the phone, you idiot? Do you know how much business I may be losing because you're a complete moron . . .?"

Two days later, Marvin suffers *another* attack and once again lapses into a coma. Dutifully, Jean calls 911. As luck would have it, the same emergency crew pulls up. As they're about to drive off with Marvin, Jean takes the driver aside and says, "Do me a favor. Watch out for potholes!"

✼ ✼ ✼

A client phones his lawyer. "I'm terribly sorry," the secretary says, "but Mr. Forsythe died this morning."

The next day, the client calls again. Patiently, the secretary reminds him the lawyer is dead. Day after day, the client keeps calling, and each time, the secretary tells him the same thing. Finally, she can't stand it anymore. "Why do you keep calling? I've told you a thousand times, Mr. Forsythe is dead!"

"I know," the client says. "I just love hearing it!"

By the year 2000, 2 out of 3 Americans could be illiterate.

It's true.

Today, 75 million adults...about one American in three, can't read adequately. And by the year 2000, U.S. News & World Report envisions an America with a literacy rate of only 30%.

Before that America comes to be, you can stop it...by joining the fight against illiteracy today.

Call the Coalition for Literacy at toll-free **1-800-228-8813** and volunteer.

Volunteer Against Illiteracy. The only degree you need is a degree of caring.